# Critical Thinking

*30 Ways to Smarter Thinking,*
*Better Problem Solving And*
*Improved Decison Making*

I0429550

# Table of Contents

# Introduction

I want to thank you and congratulate you for downloading the book, *Critical Thinking: 30 Ways to Smarter Thinking, Better Problem Solving and Improved Decision Making*. This book contains proven steps and strategies on how to improve your skill at critical thinking, many of which can be implemented easily into your regular routine.

The act of critical thinking can most easily be broken down into two core parts. The ability to properly use a group of data generating skills and the frequent use of the same to determine the best course of action in a specific situation. This skill is as important when dealing with interpersonal relationships as it is when looking inward to work through personal problems and most people don't even take the time to improve it.

However, if you spend the time and effort to train this vital skill you will begin to see results almost immediately. With proper practice and a training regimen comprised of the exercises discussed in the following chapters you will soon find you are noticing facts you would have otherwise missed and finding the solution to difficult problems with ease.

Thanks again for downloading this book, I hope you enjoy it!

# Introduction

I want to thank you and congratulate you for downloading the book, *Critical Thinking: 30 Ways to Smarter Thinking, Better Problem Solving and Improved Decision Making*. This book contains proven steps and strategies on how to improve your skill at critical thinking, many of which can be implemented easily into your regular routine.

The act of critical thinking can most easily be broken down into two core parts. The ability to properly use a group of data generating skills and the frequent use of the same to determine the best course of action in a specific situation. This skill is as important when dealing with interpersonal relationships as it is when looking inward to work through personal problems and most people don't even take the time to improve it.

However, if you spend the time and effort to train this vital skill you will begin to see results almost immediately. With proper practice and a training regimen comprised of the exercises discussed in the following chapters you will soon find you are noticing facts you would have otherwise missed and finding the solution to difficult problems with ease.

Thanks again for downloading this book, I hope you enjoy it!

are for clarifying purposes only and are the owned by the owners themselves, not affiliated with this document.

# Chapter 1: What is Critical Thinking

Critical thinking can best be defined as the intellectual process of thinking with purpose to accurately conceptualize, analyze and evaluate data that you either created through detailed observation, firsthand experience or well-reasoned thought. When done correctly it includes the detailed study of the core concepts or components of whatever is the subject of study.

The act of critical thinking can most easily be broken down into two core facets.
1.  A group of data generating skills
2.  The frequent use of the same to determine the best course of action in most situations by using a common set of procedures

The group of skills required for proper critical thinking includes inference, the ability to reach conclusions by following a line of reasoning implied by evidence. It also includes metacognition or the ability to think about and control the thought processes. Observation, analysis, interpretation and evaluation are also crucial to the critical thinking process.

When engaged in critical thinking it is important to remember a few basic facts. Gather data based on what you can perceive, do not let flights of fancy come into play. Find ways to separate the problem from its surroundings so as to study it more completely. Decide on a list of properties the correct decision would contain. Finally, hypothesize ways in which you might be able to get to the bottom of the task at hand.

Successful critical thinking includes having the ability to recognize problems and determine useful solutions. It requires the ability to gather knowledge to prioritize properly and decide which actions should take precedence in a given situation. It requires the ability to use language with accuracy and clarity and to recognize the presence or absence of relationships between logical propositions and to use those propositions to determine proper conclusions. Most importantly perhaps, it requires a persistent desire to bring under the microscope any and all supposed forms of knowledge and hold them up for closer study.

While critical thinking skills can be useful on their own they are really most effective when paired with a problem solving disposition and the decisive nature to use what is learned for the greater good. Critical thinking also requires a firm grasp of logic as well as a wide range of intellectual ideals including fairness, significance, breadth, depth, relevance, precision, accuracy, credibility and clarity.

The ways in which critical thinking skills and the ability to act based on critical thinking deductions are related are not well known. Some folks possess both in spades but having one does not always signify an abundance of the other. It is important for those looking to improve their critical thinking skills to work or both facets of the process or they will find themselves without all the tools they need to make the most of their studies.

A common method used when determining a baseline for a person's level of critical thinking is the California Measure of Mental Motivation Scale. This scale is used in academic circles to determine in broad strokes one's ability to engage and find stimulation in a variety of mentally taxing activities. The desire to think for yourself is closely linked to job performance and overall level of success. Those who experience high levels of motivation more often display problem solving skills compared to those with lower levels of motivation. As such the test is useful when aiming for self-improvement.

*Sample Questions*

1. Do they have a Fourth of July in Spain?
2. How many birthdays does the average woman have?
3. While some months have 30 days, how many months have 28?

4. A man gives a bus driver $1.50 the man is the bus driver's brother but the bus driver is not the man's brother. How is this possible?
5. Why is it not possible for a woman living in Canada to be buried in Mexico?
6. Is a woman in Arizona legally allowed to marry her widower's brother?
7. Three men play seven games of checkers and each wins the same number of times and there are no tie games. How is this possible?
8. Divide the number 40 by ½ and add 30. What is the result?
9. A woman builds a triangular house so all the sides have southern exposure. A bear walks by the house every day, what color is the bear?
10. You have four apples and you take one away, how many apples do you have?
11. You have two American coins whose total is 30 cents. If one is not a nickel, what are the two coins?
12. You walk into a room carrying a single match, inside the room is a wood burning stove and a gas lamp. What do you light first?
13. In the Bible, Moses took how many of each animal onto the ark?
14. How many three cent stamps are in a dozen?
15. How far can a woman run into the woods?

*Sample Answers*
1. Yes, it falls the day after the Third of July.
2. The woman has one birthday per year, just like every other person.
3. Every month has 28 days, only February has only 28 days.
4. The bus driver is the man's sister.
5. It is not possible because the woman is alive.
6. The woman would not be able to marry her widower's brother because she is deceased.
7. The men are capable of all winning the same number of games because they were not playing each other.

8. The answer is 110. Diving a number by ½ is the same as multiplying a number by two.
9. The bear is white because it is a polar bear. The only possible place every side of a house would have southern exposure is Antarctica.
10. You still have four apples because you are the one who took a single apple from the group.
11. The two coins are a penny and a 1972 dine with a Roosevelt imperfection which is worth exactly 29 cents. (Also a nickel and a quarter, one of the coins isn't a nickel the other is.
12. In order to light either of the other objects in the room the first thing you need to do is light the match.
13. The answer is zero. Moses didn't take animals on the ark, Noah did.
14. The correct answer is 12. There are 12 of anything in a dozen.
15. The woman can run into the woods exactly halfway as any farther and she would then be running out of the woods.

While it can be easy to write off the preceding questions as silly or useless brain teasers they all require critical thinking to complete. Another extremely important facet of critical thinking is learning to never judge a book by its cover.

# Chapter 2: Learn to Think Critically

**Determine what you hope to achieve:** A crucial part of learning to think critically is asking yourself what you hope to gain from any application of the critical thinking process. Without a firm goal in mind you won't know what to work towards or what question you want answered.

**Learn which details to pay attention to:** The most crucial aspect of critical thinking is the ability to tell which details of a particular situation are worth noting. The constant stream of information pouring out of our ever-connected world can make choosing what to focus on difficult but it is possible with practice. The best way to begin is by cultivating your intuition. If something doesn't "feel" right, it most likely isn't, listen to yourself and probe situations or problems that seem incongruous. While it will be difficult at first, the more you listen to yourself the easier listening to yourself will prove in the future.

**Determine who has the most to gain from any statement:** Whenever you read or hear an opinion based statement it can be a useful critical thinking exercise to determine who or what group or entity has the most to gain from furthering the ideas suggested in the statement. While a person saying something about which they hold a personal stake does not make that person's statement less valid on the surface, digging deeper can reveal how much bias is influencing fact. If a statement seems questionable, probe further, find the source of the facts.

**Pay attention to qualifying phrases:** Critical thinking is about more than simply training your brain, it is about training your eyes to look past the obvious and training your ears to hear what is being said and how. Many weaker arguments are couched in phrases designed to make the content more palatable. Phrases such as "I want to say" or "to be honest" can indicate it is time to reevaluate the statement by thinking critically. Using such phrases is frequently subconscious and training yourself to notice them can often give you a leg up in face to face discussions.

**Play board games:** While they might seem like kid's stuff, board games which require more skill than luck can provide player's with a wide variety of opportunities to practice their creative thinking skills. With a little searching you can find a wide variety of games aimed at adults that encourage the proper sort of thought to build alliances and maximize turn potential. It will also help you learn to use your critical thinking skills faster and on a deadline. Help your friends and family improve their skills without them even knowing.

**Know yourself:** If your goal is to truly improve your critical thinking skills one of the first things you should do is look inward critically and take stock of your own biases in thinking. Whether it is an irrational belief held over from childhood, a bias passed down from parents or a predisposition towards a particular brand of problem solving, biases are something we all have and something successful critical thinkers do their best to avoid. This can be difficult but if you take the time to cultivate viewpoints drastically different from your own then it will become easier with time.

**Practice makes perfect:** There is only one true way to improve your critical thinking skills and that is to think critically about as many things as possible as often as possible. Keeping a journal can be helpful for noting observations as they come so you can spend the time to analyze them in detail later. If you enjoy writing, then starting a blog can be a good way to focus your observations and as an added bonus the discussion you can have with those who respond to your blog can give you even more reasons to practice your critical thinking skills.

**Make use of wasted time:** While everyone is guilty of wasting time now and again, some people waste much more than others. If this describes you then make the concentrated effort to spend the time that you would usually wile away by practicing your critical thinking skills. Before you let your mind wander at the end of the day take a few moments to reflect on your day and on your strengths and weaknesses. Ask yourself when you did your most efficient thinking and decide if there were any moments where you could have used critical thinking more effectively.

**Wrestle with a problem a day:** As a mental exercise to improve critical thinking it can be beneficial to choose a problem every morning before the day has had a chance to kick into full swing. Then, as you find time throughout the day, break the problem down into its basic components and determine the most efficient way of solving each one. Really study the problem so you understand all the information that is provided, Analyze and interpret your findings and then evaluate possible solutions. Start with an easy problem or even a word problem you find online, before long your mind will be a problem solving machine.

**Focus on intellectual ideals:** The concepts of fairness, significance, breadth, depth, relevance, precision, accuracy, credibility and clarity are all key to improving your critical thinking skills but it can be difficult to try and improve at utilizing so many things at once. Instead, try and focus on ways to improve at utilizing one each week. Breaking the list down into manageable chunks not only makes progress more manageable but allows you greater freedom to experience the breadth of each concept and over time understand how they all work together to improve critical thinking.

**Understand your emotions:** Whenever you feel a particularly strong emotion either positive or negative it can be a helpful mental exercise to take stock of the situation as it applies to the emotion and break down specifically why you are feeling the way you feel. Analyzing this data when you have access to all of the details can be helpful when you are eventually faced with a series of events which you know and the emotional response of another person which you can see but are unclear as to how one relates to another. Practicing on your own emotional responses will give you greater empathy towards others.

**Analyze group influences:** Much like when analyzing your own emotions, analyzing the influences the social groups you are a part of place upon you can be a useful mental exercise to increase your critical thinking skills. Taking a look at your behavior and how individual actions are condoned or discouraged in various social groups can give you a clearer example of how other people react in certain situations and why. Every group espouses its own unique rules and guidelines that influence action, understanding a variety of such rules and guidelines can make critical thinking easier.

**Ask more questions:** When working to improve your critical thinking skills it can be beneficial to question everything. Start inward by questioning why you think you know what you know and work outward from there. The human brain works by making assumptions about the world around it and by questioning these assumptions as they come you can learn to more naturally question assumptions that may arise when dealing with potential problems in the wild. Questioning assumptions can be considered the bedrock of the critical thinking process and it should be practiced at every opportunity.

**Dig deeper with presented information:** Rather than taking information presented to you as fact, another useful critical thinking exercise can be to decide not to take benign information presented to you at face value. While it is uncommon for information presented by family and friends to be maliciously misleading, tracking down the source of presented information can make it easier to do the same when it matters. Questionable information may be difficult to verify and having extra practice can make the task much easier to complete when required. Keep in mind that any form of media contains at least one type of bias and never trust the internet to be bias free.

**Develop a critical thinking disposition:** As an exercise to increase your ability to think critically it can be beneficial to approach any new situation by analyzing it using your critical thinking skills first. This will allow you to both learn what sort of problems are best solved using critical thinking and to get in the habit of using critical thinking skills as second nature. While not every problem can be solved by critical thinking, learning the difference can be useful. Only when you begin to apply your critical thinking skills without consciously thinking about them will you be able to consider yourself a true critical thinker.

# Chapter 3: Advanced Tips for Successful Critical Thinking

**Focus on thinking farther ahead:** While many people think one or two steps ahead of their current actions, successful critical thinkers get in the habit of thinking four or five steps ahead. While such successful planning has many obvious benefits, one of the most practical is the way this habit will improve your critical thinking skills. Thinking further ahead will make it much easier to work through the analysis portion of any problem as by seeing the beginning of the problem you are already focusing on the end.

**Read more:** Reading as habit has fallen by the wayside for society at large which is a shame for few passive activities can have such a profound impact on critical thinking skills. While reading focus on honing your critical thinking skills by putting yourself in the narrator's shoes and attempting to deduce what they are going to do next. Practically every chapter will give you new opportunities to practice and by the end of a series you will be transferring your skills into the real world without even trying. Bonus points for reading Sherlock Holmes and learning by example as well.

**Set aside time to practice:** While building your skills as time allows or when the need arises will work for a time, to continue taking your critical thinking skills to the next level you need to set aside a portion of every day to solely focus on improvement. While this practicing time could simply be spent reading and questioning the actions of the protagonist it could just as easily be spent debating with others in person or online or simply listening to the problems of your friends and family and using your critical thinking skills to help find solutions.

**Get out and exercise:** While popular culture would have you believe that brains and brawn don't mix, in reality the opposite is true. Studies have shown that as little as twenty minutes of physical activity can help improve both brain activity and function. While this doesn't mean you have to get out and run a marathon, try taking the dog for a walk around the block, you will be surprised at how much more alert you will feel. As an added bonus while you walk you can practice any of the mental exercises suggested here for maximum benefit.

**Eat more brain foods:** While it can be easy to overlook, the type of foods you eat can play a major role in your ability to effectively practice critical thinking. Quality foods to reach for when your brain needs a boost include protein such as nuts, brown rice or salmon, and fruits including blueberries and avocados. Leafy greens including broccoli and cabbage contain lots of folate which has been shown in studies to noticeably improve memory by increasing blood flow to the brain. Likewise, foods that are high in fats, salt and starch can leave you feeling dull.

**Improve your journaling:** If you have been practicing correct critical thinking methods then you will already be keeping a journal, now it is time to use it to the fullest. Use some of the time you have set aside for practice to write out a situation you felt was emotionally significant and break it down using the following suggestions. First, describe the situation in detail. Second, honestly write down what you did in response. Third, analyze the specifics of the situation being as precise as possible. Fourth, assess the situation and determine if you took the correct course of action and, if not, what the correct response would have been.

**Improve yourself:** Now that you have worked on improving your grasp of intellectual ideals it is time to turn that facet of study inward and focus on improving your personal traits. Whether it is something easy to work on such as perseverance, or something more nebulous such as humility, bending your will towards this pursuit will force you to become more in tune with yourself and aware of your successes and failures. Only when you are completely aware of every facet of yourself will you be able to ignore all your biases.

**Choose to see the world differently:** While it can be easy to understand empirically that everyone person has a unique point of view that may not necessarily reflect our own, it can be much more difficult to force our minds to see things from that different perspective. If you have been practicing the exercises recommended in chapter two, then you will understand the biases you hold and how they affect the way you view the world. Now you should attempt to take this a step farther and try and put yourself in someone else's shoes and think about how their differences alter the way they interact with the world.

**Practice Deep Analysis:** At the point in your studies where analyzing data as you receive it becomes second nature, it is time to begin attempting to take your analysis deeper. For practice take a look back at early journal entries and analyze your analysis as an exercise in spotting otherwise hidden biases. Breakdown any assumptions you might have previously used and try to determine why you thought to use them and what concepts you were really trying to convey. Using a deeper form of analysis on your own thoughts can lead to surprising results.

**Keep it simple:** While eventually you will be able to use the creative thinking method to get to the bottom of any sticky situation, it can be another thing entirely to keep the process of doing so from turning into a relative quagmire. The next time you attempt a go at critical thinking, approach the task critically. Ask yourself which steps you can combine or how you can go about reaching the same conclusion in half the time. By focusing on reducing the process as much as possible you make it easier for it to become second nature.

**Avoid ego enhancing behavior:** With time you will be able to use your critical thinking skills to evaluate the actions you and others take and determine the root cause of the action whether it came about as the result of internal or external factor. Actions taken as the result of a need to protect the ego are both unproductive biases which can negatively affect our ability to think critically when coming from ourselves and unneeded variables when determining actions in others. Take the time to become aware of these insidious factors and avoid them whenever possible.

**Keep a balanced perspective:** As you become more adept at thinking critically it will slowly but surely become easier and easier to maintain a balanced perspective when in the midst of chaos. As you internalize the critical thinking process you will find that it is easier to make quick decisions in the moment and that they are likely to be the right ones when it counts. Cultivate this ability and make a concentrated effort to apply your critical thinking skills quickly when in situations where time is not a factor so it is easier to do so when it is.

**Prune your word choice:** Often times the act of critical thinking can be thought of as a sort of dialogue you have with yourself in regards to a specific problem or topic. Ensuring that the way you speak to yourself is productive and does nothing to reinforce negative thoughts or behaviors can streamline your critical thinking process and make the individual steps much easier to complete. What's more, reinforcing a negative self-image can create judgement biases where you second guess yourself even if you were on the right track all along. Trust your critical thinking skills and reinforce that trust by talking to yourself in a positive way.

**Restructure illogical thinking:** Once critical thinking has become a force of habit it can be beneficial to use the critical thinking process to evaluate other thought processes for efficiency and results. Only when critical thinking has influenced your broader manner of thought is it effective to use it to weed out other thought processes that might be hiding behind bias or inefficiency. Performing this self-evaluation will ultimately lead to a more efficient method of critical thinking in the long run. Pay special attention to instances of illogical thinking as they can easily spread and become incorrect assumptions.

**Develop foresight:** Everyone has the ability to predict the likely outcome of an event based on past experience, good critical thinkers harness this ability whenever possible and do their best to nurture it. As an exercise read about a series of events and attempt to predict what will happen next.

# Conclusion

Thank you again for downloading this book! I hope it was able to aid you in your quest to master the practice of critical thinking. Using the process of critically thinking takes time and practice but if you persevere you will find your mental acuity honed and your observational skills and memory heightened. Continue to use critical thinking in your everyday life and to make a concentrated effort to set time aside to practice each week.

The next step is to continue using critical thinking as much as possible in as wide a variety of situations as possible. Critical thinking is like a muscle; it needs constant exercise to grow. Only through constant practice will this unique skill improve so continue working at it, all the people you ultimately help with thank you.

Finally, if you enjoyed this book, then I'd like to ask you for a favor, would you be kind enough to leave a review for this book on Amazon? It'd be greatly appreciated!

www.ingramcontent.com/pod-product-compliance
Lightning Source LLC
Chambersburg PA
CBHW072015280526
45788CB00005B/2061